Bb Trumpet 1

AS WE SLEEP

.yan Meeboer

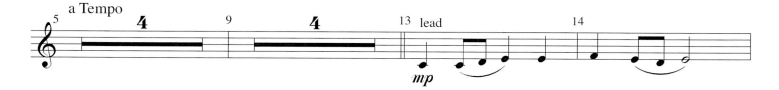

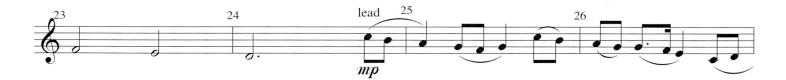

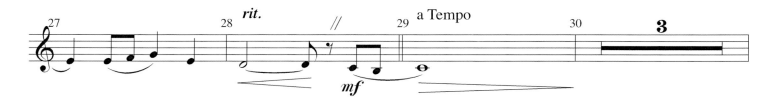

Bb Trumpet 2

AS WE SLEEP

Ryan Meeboer

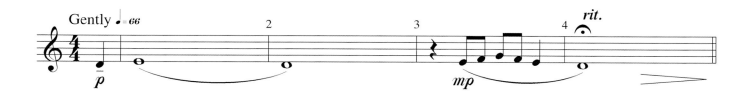

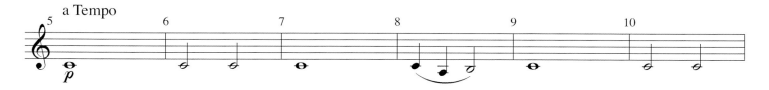

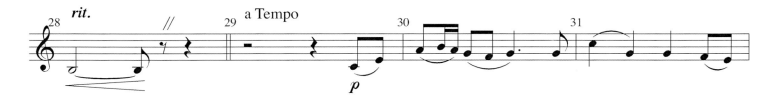

F Horn

AS WE SLEEP

Ryan Meeboer

Trombone

AS WE SLEEP

Ryan Meeboer

Tuba

AS WE SLEEP

Ryan Meeboer

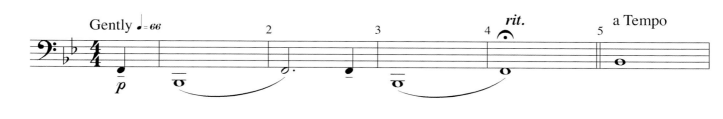

EIGHTH NOTE ♪ PUBLICATIONS

As We Sleep

Ryan Meeboer

This lyrical piece is a modern lullaby. It begins with a peaceful feeling and slowly builds into a beautiful, chorale-like section, reflecting the wonderful dreams we have as we fall into our deepest sleep.

The horn is first to play the main melody of the piece at measure 5. In measures 8 and 12, have the support players bring out the motion in their parts, as the melody comes to a rest. This will allow the piece to continue its motion, and avoid the feel of whole note gaps. The same will happen in measures 16 and 20.

As the counter melody is introduced in the horn at 13, be sure it doesn't dominate, since it is meant to compliment the main melody performed by the trumpet.

At 21 the trombone takes over the melody with the other voices supporting.

As the opening melody returns at measure 29, Trumpet 2 will have the opportunity to shine. Since this is new material, it should be clearly heard over the main melody.

Ryan Meeboer is a music educator, who obtained his degree through the Ontario Institute for Studies in Education at the University of Toronto. As a composer, he has written and arranged many pieces for concert band, jazz band, and small ensembles. His young band piece, *Last Voyage of the Queen Anne's Revenge*, has been well received by performers, educators, and audiences, and his pieces are starting to be found on festival and contest lists. As a performer, he has had experience in several groups, including concert and stage bands, chamber choir, vocal jazz ensemble, acoustic duets, and the Hamilton based swing group, "The Main Swing Connection".

Ryan began studying music at the age of seven through private guitar lessons. During his years in elementary and secondary school, he gained experience in several families of instruments. Focusing on music education and theory (including composition and orchestration), he attended McMaster University to achieve his honours degree in music. Ryan is currently a teacher for the Halton District School Board in Ontario, where he continues to compose and arrange.

Please contact the composer if you require any further information about this piece
or his availability for commissioning new works and appearances.

ryan.meeboer@enpmusic.com

ISBN: 9781771578646   COST: $15.00   DIFFICULTY RATING: Easy-Medium
CATALOG NUMBER: BQ222541   DURATION: 2:40   Brass Quintet

www.enpmusic.com

AS WE SLEEP

Ryan Meeboer